RARE EARTH

poems by

Kelsi Vanada

Finishing Line Press
Georgetown, Kentucky

RARE EARTH

for my family

ACKNOWLEDGMENTS

Grateful acknowledgement is made to the editors of the following journals,
where versions of some of these poems first appeared: *Bennington Review,
The Iowa Review, Columbia Poetry Review, Court Green, New Delta Review,
Guesthouse, The Des Moines Register, The Bridge* (journal of the Danish
American Heritage Society), *The Journal,* and *Prelude.*

My thanks to all who have taught me, and to all who read versions of these
poems along their way. I am grateful also to the Danish American Heritage
Society and the Baltic Centre for Writers and Translators for their support as
this collection came together.

Publisher: Leah Maines
Editor: Christen Kincaid
Cover Art: Ingalls family archive
Author Photo: Patrick Ploschnitzki
Cover Design: Elizabeth Maines McCleavy

Printed in the USA on acid-free paper.
Order online: www.finishinglinepress.com
            also available on amazon.com

Author inquiries and mail orders:
Finishing Line Press
P. O. Box 1626
Georgetown, Kentucky 40324
U. S. A.

Table of Contents

"The memory house too airy & blown out to hold more"
—E. Sikelianos

"Whoever rides into the scene changes it"
—C.D. Wright

"There's a weed whose name I've meant all summer to find out"
—C. Phillips

BE WILDER

here I am looking
for points of arrest.
would've done as well
rides in on the back of it
and starts to give.
here's a quote
about the greatest of all
shrubs and branches:
they winced in the heat.
saw fit to break,
slid down the pediment
(me, in the pediment).
settled on that technical
clicking. made it all sake.
my little rabbit/racket
(the ground meanwhile
may leap into the sky).
telescopic, the gathering.
the earth like blankets
in my arms. it took a bit
to loosen the threads
at the heart of the old
whistle. I had to pretend
I wasn't mourning.
I say night never ends.
still barely extant
the overall furniture.
look how small
the evergreen bushes behind me
are.

THIS IS THE HORSE POEM I'VE BEEN TRYING TO WRITE

Photograph circa 1944: this horse's head's cut off. Its hooves are, too. Who manned this camera? Central: my great-uncle Eldon, Marie's little brother, two years old, astride the horse. His hair's so blonde it's nonexistent white in the light of day, or of the camera. Shiny bright spot where a boy's forehead should be. His ear to her coat the only touch-point between him and the Lakota woman he sits behind, riding double with her. *Mrs. Sam Butcher*, he tells me when he sends the photograph. *She was our sheepherder when Dad ran sheep on rented reservation pastureland.* Holding the colorless print, I can't meet his eyes. Her face's blurred, flaw in the developing, or she's turning away from the camera's snap, like its moment came a half-second before she'd planned, or she's speaking to Eldon, turning to face him: don't fall off. My great-grandfather's brand is on the horse's shoulder's flesh. Behind its flanks a man's torso-less legs: feet hidden in tallgrass, his head's blocked by the woman, did he just set Eldon on the horse for the photograph? In the sky, gray, winged specks're surely not birds. The Cheyenne River Reservation's just a mile from Faith.

A RANCH CALLED BRUISE

I stream back I cannot   help
but pick up a house as I go
and other things of that   nature
I'm the ghost   who haunts it

every single expression keep
hushing   I didn't mean
to meet you in my dream

can't work toward   or at you
but finally   a cool wind
off the dam   look
what color it is   now
as tender as ever it was

whoever lived in the house
before you   must have been the same
don't let it tell you   anything to   ears

A LONG, NARROW MARK ON A SURFACE

bulb, I thought. or
maybe bare brightness.
afar is tough
to hold, see rightly.
it backs me,
bending over hill-light and
head-light. enough to say
I've been zinging:
you made me zing.
I'll bet you everything
is slightly curved, a stretch
afar off. (here it's left over
from the road. distilled
just once in this line of yearning
trees. land-hitting).
I mean the soul-bulb,
fleshy water-log, soaked
till planted. a streaming
tangle.
I'd capture its sharpness
with other materials.
all fading nicely at the very
leaf.

FIELD, BOOK-NAME, CINQUEFOIL

My grandmother's eyes are closed in almost every photo of her that exists. Here, she must be two, holding out a bottle to a lamb that meets Marie before a shrub. A lilac, maybe, but not in spring. In bare Dakota dirt. In this, it's her wedding, she alone in the party gathered at the altar has eyes closed. It's the official photo, it's in the family albums. In the Faith newspaper too, though harder to tell the angle of her lids given the yellowed pixilation of the printing. Then in full color, she squats beside a clump of yellow flowers, eyes shut to them. Her daughter's squinting on her knee, her son's behind her, standing, squinting too. Is it a gravesite on the prairie? No headstone, but the grass here's greener than it is around the group. I'm in one, too, sitting on her lap outside the clothing store she ran in town, looking over at my brother goofing off in a propeller cap. It's summer, I'm sunburned and twisting my hair in my fingers, it's probably even green from all the chlorine in the pool. This time, my little sister has the closed eyes. Gramma's wearing sunglasses, so I can't see hers again. Today she's eighty-one, photos of her appeared on the online profile she hasn't touched in many years, though people still keep commenting on them. On one, my mom writes that my Grampa's eyes were always on her.

touch a thing to keep it
in its place

the years he spent his arm
inside a cow

feeling for a calf

THE WEED OF THE DAY IS PURSLANE

we loved a sewing metaphor   no more
not stitched but   rubbing
this bad penny   till its sheen is off
can't fondle it more   its copper can't hurt
my hands together   my looking down
coin fallen out and lost   to me somewhere
weight so small   I don't miss it
can't say I never did   when it had sheen
I missed   all that first lushest
even this   small burned hole
is ringed with melt   though there's
a bit of loss in it   a speckle of grass
may stab it through   what's felt
in the green globe   doesn't need proved

ALL MY DEFAULT IMAGES

Damn it, Great-Grandfather, you're so quiet I can't hear you in this photograph. A dramatic entrance I did not intend: I meant to write about how Katrine's plant grows straight vertical. *Whenever,* his sister always said in place of *when.* Time opening to include him in that *ever.* A detail he'd forgotten since leaving Faxe, but how would I know. In the photograph these characters don't speak to one another. (Small noise this woman makes in anyone's memory.) A fruit to be explained: it is only in leaf growth that the photograph differs from the scene, leaves in her full hands now. I told no one about it, it's just in a picture. Katrine's plant. I heard the eye catches dark patches in paintings or photographs first. Surveying her brother's visit to the old farm in Denmark, his first in forty years. A figure in each pane. Nobody knows they should have let me in on the speech between siblings. I mean hidden by them.

COW SENSE

This family just might have more cattle photographs
than folks. Whole sleeves of them by year, clear back
to Kastor of Valley Mound, the oldest registered Angus bull
anyone ranching who now remembers can remember.
Folders full of names like Windy Star, Ingalls Special 5, Big
Fortune. And there were the almost-pets: the docile bull
that followed Dale for scratches behind the ears. The steer
Duane dressed up. I had cattle, too: the cow with ear tag 342
laid on her calf till it was dead. At auctions later their issue
turned tuition dollars. The calves in head gates I have sprayed
with flea dip watching testicles yanked out and slashed,
trailing long red cords. *Good eye appeal's* what Grampa says.
Licorices sucked and socketed. *If you select for just one trait
too hard, you sacrifice another.* The breed's in a good place.

MY DEFECT

work is meticulous, but homemade like how
we say our clothes are patched and worn
but clean. I say my fiber is fine,
may shift expectations
exceptions. I have thought of very little else.
fiber/flower. world-weary bloom.
your petals are patches I'm holding
under no certain tutelage.
if a tear throw it out.
the fiber machine is to blame. these flaws
are marring a known strictness or stricture.

I'm drawn into a scene. meaning I appear
refluent as it appears to me.
drawing the stroke out, throwing it
out, drawing it through.
along the way your face changes. I hoped
to erase the hand on these materials.
precision: of course I feel it.
the boards are pressed
we can raise them now. just.
show how to untake a done defected thing.
show a little world off
in the material of it.

AFTER A FASHION

when trying to explain for him she said it's like on a sunny day with wind. you take your sweater. on again, off. again. it could be he relied on her. her blue-and-red chest of drawers from Norway. even in the 8mm home movies you can see. he's not going anywhere. he's parked at the ocean side. or he's jump-cutting to the next scene, his little daughter jumping. for the camera. it all moves a little fast. beggars their marks. one yellow screen on the black-and-white, and they're gone. or maybe a sheen of forest through the windshield (through the lens) (through the eye) comes flitting. they're young in the movies, though as she says their dress makes them look like the previous generation. the same boy had two lives. or three. his daughter had language ears. couldn't read her own lips in the movies. is this part in color. that's how she said I remember it. her mark on the movie is a jagged, bouncing line. she moves so fast she's a mass of light hair in the corner. of the frame. maybe she dropped the camera or maybe her language. wasn't enough. to own his printing company, those giant rolls of paper in the country. in the business.

when I went back to the prairie I
couldn't find the
blade of grass/bootjack/swaying shack

couldn't even find
the Ball glass/heifer smash

it was a beautiful day to

DREAM EVENT: WE'RE VISITING THE RANCH HOUSE

Dad's at the kitchen sink, grouching at the vegetables he's pulled from the garden. Ripping open pea pods to find them black inside, squeezing zucchini to find them soft and rotted; he throws each vegetable roughly into the left side of the sink, saying: *I used to make good food from this garden and now it will make everyone sick.* The furniture's rearranged, and some of it I don't recognize; that glider rocker with the squeak that put us to sleep is gone. Outside it's turned night; I try to catch up to a group of people moving over the yard, singing in one of the Siouan languages. They have no light with them; the yard is the out-and-out dark of the plains: I know they're there because of their singing and the presence of the mass of them, breathing together and rustling the night. Make me part of it. The song is "Night of Peace" but I can't join in: I don't know the words and now the people are gone. Day again: I step onto the back porch to find that new buildings have cropped up behind the house; now two apartments hang, half-completed, over the ranch. A strip of plastic tarp snaps a report from a window hole on one of the top floors, hundreds of feet above. There's a new outbuilding, too: low, built rough of old wood, but it isn't storing cattle or feed, just more building supplies. Inside the house, I find Dale's mind has gone. He's not just forgetful; this time he's doddering. He sits on the edge of the bed, still in boots, riveted on nothing: I've never seen him so stock still. *Sort the black Angus from the red Angus,* he's muttering. He's never run red Angus at all.

NOTICEABLE DISTANCE

we stood for hours in the gathering
heat. a wind could draw it off.
if I say it was a little house you
know. alluded to in the middle distance:
rimrock, posthole, spindrift. little
brushfire in the trees, smoke in the nose.
we like what we are used to; the prairies
are used to fire. burn it. again.
go on quietly, taking a done thing.
in our sight a little extra shine,
a coloring we can't name. burning up
our technical progressive thought.

night glows like day. we are a burning
people. only our guilt stops us
thinking straightening is best. straining.
what to make of our insistence on
insistence. that the prairie burn. our
dream value land of many uses we gather
to watch it burn. we arrive
facing; the blaze gets us talking. how
does it get us? it's done us in, I'll tell you.
the land and noticeable distance,
offering as one way
sky's enflamed delight.
can't be unlit. spit in the fire
crackles, it's close enough to singe. sing.

OFF-CENTURY

I'd thought to narrate a couple moments in a slew of sounds, but a break in the loop means there's no loop. It's a brittle prairie. How to indicate an understanding of a composition, or hand-wash simplicity and hang-dry it. Here I'm putting in a name: Anna. I'm making an arc across the Atlantic (or Anna is). She's like giving a gift, it's good to have her name. Sing us that run-down, played-out, light-on-things: a hay-green grave-making high glow. Wild in the back of the back forty is Anna. But she's Ida. Wanted to be photographed before she lost her beauty. Didn't she fit into the family? Stranded into Anna's roam? Norwegian was close enough (I think) to understand her portly Danish husband in the dark. In America. Straighten syllables, gut the glottal, Anna/Ida picked a place. Anna/Ida knew the other's face.

NOTHING FOR IT

the junk rotting in the dump in the draw
a pelvis plucked from a sage clump on Bone Hill
the mineral rights they did not own
a bit of barrel from the Benson place still
the missile silos buried under gumbo in the 60s
the toddler who drowned in the well on the
original homestead

I AM BOUND TO TELL YOU

we fix the boundaries.
it's fallen to us to fix them, all trusses
and leftovers and sticks.
the land is bound to shift,
the posts to sink and lean
and wires to sag. we drag
a wire in the dust behind the truck
to draw it from its coil.
it tries to bound away, goes straight.

at the midpoint of the boundary,
where your place bounds on mine,
we meet and look
across the line and both fix right.
we stretch the wire tight, we
splice the breaks with bits of spare.
then bind it to the posts, and sense
each other through the line.
not mine. we're both bound up
in this. we're grabbing at the pieces
pushing from our grasp.
we'll insist on *we*, imagine
we can keep it up. homebound,
some say. I'm bound for I don't know.

MAKE BELIEVE

We were what anyone would call obsessed, reenacting
that colonial crossing the family always deemed
heroic. Yes, Ingalls is my mother's maiden name.
A Radio Flyer our covered wagon—if we were nice
we might convince my brother to pull us in it westward
through the yard. As Pa, he had a wooden gun for shooting game.
I, always Laura—she was wildest. My sister, Baby Carrie—
I could boss her. I hated beef jerky, but it seemed authentic.
So did our fringed vests. We stole carrots from the garden
and ate them with the dirt still crunching in our teeth.
A blue tarp for the rivers we forded—all this caught
on film. As a teen, I exchanged my gingham bonnet
for dying of dysentery in a game I played white-
knuckled. Just like those books, this tells you what I did.

THESE THINGS COME INTO MY MIND FROM TIME TO TIME

While Dale and Duane rotated cattle in the pastures to keep from overgrazing (Buffalo Grass forms a solid turf but can accommodate wildflowers) and mowed in front of the ranch house (Blue Grama grows as a bunch grass) and set Daniel to mowing around the trees in the tree patch (Little Bluestem is Wiregrass to Dale) and cultivated alfalfa in a few pastures and made grass hay in others (Crested Wheatgrass is used for winter forage, though protein supplements are required for livestock) and cut (Orchard Grass, according to Teri, is kind of a weed) and raked (like Cheatgrass, a word you need to swear in front of, Dale says, because it invades the alfalfa) and dried (Brome Grass is a tame grass that can grow in waste places) and baled it (Needlegrass, also called Wiregrass, or Whitegrass, or Prairie Three-awn, is an indicator of overgrazed rangeland) into round bales (Western Wheatgrass has strong spreading rhizomes and greens up in March or early April) which my mother painted into her ranch landscapes (Indian Grass has been confused with Tall Oats Grass, and is relished by livestock) and which browned, sagged,

and were unrolled in winter (Prairie Beardgrass is also known as Little Bluestem) except for when they had to buy hay when the summer had been too dry (Side-oats Grama helped recover the grasslands following the drought of the 1930s, Howard told me), I plucked grasses (Turkey Claw is what Duane calls Big Bluestem) and put them in my mouth to taste their growing because somewhere I'd heard it was a country thing to do (Junegrass has no leaves on the stem, is distinct from June Grass, is sometimes called Poverty Grass or White Oat Grass, and is easily confused with Red Fescue), and my siblings and I plucked more grasses (Porcupine Grass is also called Strictus) by handfuls and braided them into long ropes (Green Foxtail is a heavy seed producer but a poor competitor unless in dense stands) adding new grasses when we got to the ends until we had great coils long enough for jump roping except the grass ropes were too fragile to move the air (Pigeon Grass is what Bernice calls Green Foxtail, though its other names) and next day were too brittle to use even for binding more grasses (are Green Bristle Grass, Wild Millet, and Bottle Grass) into my own small bales.

the sky looks hammered flat
out

I saw a dead goose here once,
under this power line

it was quite

I RECUSE MY SET PIECE

we are in the soft warm center
of summer. you come closer
and say oh, it's colors: they get
on the wind like a scent. oriole or
redwing, you hardly knew.
my reaction's admirable, too:
watch me in the blind I'm
showing off mine. every single
one keep shining, side by each
so we have them to hand.

twenty sightings says
the life I've got I want.
or we're much put upon by sky.
under it I saw blight on all things,
all useless in the waver:
a small tree standing in a shorn
field, shorn forest. it was a birch.

what else to say beyond what you.
in a string of slow names I found yours
to make a tongue turn thunder.
joint-trunked. balled-up. best bunched.
I know we use what we need now.
time to set this set piece down.

I AM AT A PAIN TO REPRESENT THE FOLLOWING ARRAY

After the house burned in '82 I know the dog Blackie whined
and pawed the hot ash till they had to put her away.
On the ranch *put down* or *away* was another way to say
shot. As a teen I put away a prairie dog. I'd been convinced
they were vermin whose holes could take down a cow
worth a few thousand dollars. Maybe that was true.
In any case, I held and fired the .22. You could say, too,
that the boy Daniel who was not my cousin put away
my Uncle Duane. You might call him my uncle's foster son.
He was seventeen when he did it, so you might not call
him a boy. In the end the courts did not. I've tried
but there is no other way to say: one day
he waited at the window of the farmhouse they shared
and aimed and put him away. I think of them often.

MOVES THROUGH ERROR

Driving down the hill in the truck, he pitched around a turn, skidding on the washboard dirt road. Driving back to the ranch, he jackknifed around a hairpin turn in the truck and drove into the ravine. Driving around a sharp turn in the dirt road to the cabin, the truck spun out past a stand of fir trees on the edge. He raced down the mountain road from the cabin, hit a patch of loose gravel around a

turn, and the truck pitched down. Heading back to the ranch after a weekend at the family A-frame in the Black Hills, he drove the truck around a bend and pitched off. On the way down the mountain road, he drove the snowmobile around a hairpin turn, skidded out on the packed snow, and flew into the gorge. He pitched to the right, over the side of the cliff and into the valley, on his four-wheeler. The cab hung suspended over the edge of the drop-off. The vehicle was totaled, the bend marked. Correction: hairpin turn, he pitching off?

a piece of trash leapt
at the side of the road

and this time it didn't turn mud
it turned gold

CHECK MY WORK

in the county book   their stories
don't say the road's smooth

Marie insisted they fully   weren't using
the right word   stamp flood   full stop
what is a right   pace for a rancher

dear Marie   this is an immigrant
letter   lost at a sort of   rushed end

alive in the air   catch
a hand to your knee
sleep   in the sloped room

check my work   I remained
I buttoned down   I kept

MY LEAN-TO

one lean-to wall gives on
another. at a certain pitch.
onto one shoulder (they call it)
or another. is my lean-to tenable.
at its pitch. completely polished or
clinking into place exactly. how
much room is there within it
for another. my lean-to requires no nails;
can it lean on you. if you pitch
I will respond; I may lean one way
as in no one way. I may lean into or away.
a lattice (I call it)—put this in the past tense,
it should have been. how far over
can one be pitched before one pitches. over.

THE STORY JUMPS A LITTLE, EXPECTING YOU CAN FOLLOW

it is needful to burn and so I am. burning trash. with every burn barrel
billow I'm split. old life and old. I pitch in songbooks, thin linens. I
won't write how thatched roofs used to hold down earth. plume straight
ascends. yard cut by light. growing pressure. the old farm in my head.
old companion anger. rising. the land I'd have farmed. exchanged for
this patch I can't get purchase on. this landscape dust I'm swallowing. a
whole worn thing. (drape the wheat fields of Faxe around me like a flag
against the wind on the Dakota plains). I'm playing with a new word,
dragging it. through my old language and scraping up sounds. like
Gefion's plough through Sjælland to carve it out. her sons turned oxen
to do the work. my sons and daughters turned American. these cowboy
children of mine surprise me. what is a place of birth. a handhold. a
hand up, handed down. the old country swells in my head. and so it
will. and so it goes. also mine, and mine, and mine. can the pressure. be
relieved. with my way I'd stop thinking of it. there I've said it. no place.
to keep my mind. who else is having trouble with thistle.

RARE EARTH

I have a sliver of qualm.
that's in 3D you know,
meaning you can see it all
over me, that river smell
murky on me, like you
on that rock above seeing
me or from a limestone
cliff, could be. the sliver
is you're there, is
not sure where to put
your foot. in the night.
in the hotel. on me. in
the rock's spine. on mine.

ROSA MAY DELANEY INGALLS:
TOWNSHIP 13. RANGE 11. SECTION 5.

she said been working this quarter
of a quarter section
all my life. she said what
she meant: I want to buy it.
I want it with mine.
no improvements she said
have been made. I could ink it in
the plat book, where it shows
his name there: Prattle.
no one could find him
but there it stands, his
unknown name scrawled
in that cramped square.
just four lines, she said
it was evidence.

maps rolled down like fabric bolts
when the town was platted.
when was it platted. whose
name was first to homestead.
shift the outline only
40 acres she said by his name,
it's my work. come out
where you exist, was her cry.
he made it up, she said.
she decided. she ran her cattle.
set it down in plat. she said she said
she thinks him a gap.
no way out of that.

RETURN

is always where I've left
return, brackish
with one more night.
evening
the edges, it draws me
on. which is to say, to seek
to mend again
a rend
in the keeping of a handy
structure.
in turn, there is no
turn.

THE NAME'LL HAVE TO DO ME

at this little house
on this prairie
the Ingalls family
cut up a beef

Kelsi Vanada grew up in Monument, Colorado. She holds MFAs in Poetry (Iowa Writers' Workshop, 2016) and Literary Translation (University of Iowa, 2017). She translates from Spanish and collaboratively from Swedish, and her poems and translations have been published most recently in *The Literary Review, Bennington Review, The Iowa Review, Tupelo Quarterly,* and *Anomaly.* Her translation of *The Eligible Age* by Berta García Faet was published in 2018 with Song Bridge Press; a translation of Sergio Espinosa's *hacia la mudez* is forthcoming from Veliz Books.

Kelsi was an ALTA Travel Fellow in 2016. She was awarded a residency in 2018 at the Baltic Centre for Writers and Translators in Visby, Sweden for her translations (with the poet) of Marie Silkeberg's *Atlantis,* for which she won the American-Scandinavian Foundation's 2018 Nadia Christensen Translation Prize. Kelsi is the Program Manager of the American Literary Translators Association (ALTA) and lives in Tucson, Arizona.

www.ingramcontent.com/pod-product-compliance
Lightning Source LLC
LaVergne TN
LVHW051611080426
835510LV00020B/3236